LADDERS UP

LADDERS
UP TO HEAVEN

by

Elizabeth Urch

PART 1
Christmas

By the same author
BE STILL MY SOUL

Published by
ARTHUR JAMES LIMITED
THE DRIFT EVESHAM WORCS.
ENGLAND

First Edition 1980

© Elizabeth Urch

All rights reserved by the publishers
Arthur James Limited of Evesham, Worcs., England

British Library Cataloguing in Publication Data

Urch, Elizabeth
  Ladders up to heaven.
  Christmas
  1. Christian Literature
  I. Title
  808.8   BR53

ISBN 0–85305–226–3

Produced by Print WorkShop of Bath
and
Photoset by Kelly Typesetting Limited
Bradford on Avon, Wiltshire.

Printed in Great Britain by
John Wright & Sons, Ltd., at the Stonebridge Press, Bristol

Though Christ a thousand times
In Bethlehem be born,
If He's not born in thee
Thy soul is still forlorn

Angelus Silesius (1624–1677)

For Emma

IT WAS THE LAST CHRISTMAS EVE of the seventies. The sun shone gloriously on the West Sands of St. Andrews where I spent about an hour contemplating among other things the beauty and poetry of this historic University town which held so much personal meaning and so many different memories for me.

Legend has told of the arrival here of Regulus or Rule, abbot of the monastery of Patras, who came carrying the relics of the apostle St. Andrew. And there is the compelling silhouette of a skeleton of a fourteenth century cathedral—in fact the only Gothic cathedral to overlook the sea—in this case the North Sea.

The town is the seat of the third oldest university in Britain, a centre of teaching and scholarship still maintaining its link between University and Church. Normally in term time the streets of St. Andrews are ablaze with the warm scarlet flannel gowns of the undergraduates. On Sundays they fill the ancient College Chapel of St. Salvator's and then walk along the old harbour wall for the traditional Sunday Pier Walk.

But on this Christmas Eve most of the undergraduates were home and I was alone on the West Sands, thinking of how deeply I loved this cosmopolitan place with all its natural beauty, legend, history and its poetic and academic atmosphere.

I came on another lone soul, similarly clad in anorak and warm woollen ski hat, protection against the cold wind blowing in from the North Sea, which raced wild and sparkling and beautiful. As she passed, I smiled a greeting and she said, "It all helps to get this mad, mad world in perspective, doesn't it?" How right she was.

I need not have walked alone that Christmas Eve for back at the University Chaplain's House I had left most of my happy family gathered for the festive season. But I wanted to be alone with my own thoughts for a while as I tried to imagine what the coming decade might bring. I wasn't quite sure about the future in my profession as Head Teacher of a rural school, as for several months I had suffered a throat malady which could put my career in jeopardy. I felt I was giving in to worry which I have always regarded as a negative emotion.

Why should I spoil this lovely day with negative emotions? If I were going to be able to continue in my post, then all the worry would have been needless. If, however, my teaching days were nearly over, and my casual broadcasting episodes were coming to a premature end, why spoil the fruitful days left by worrying about it before the final blow fell?

My mind went back to another day many years ago, when I had walked the same beach on a similarly clear, sunlit April day. That time, however, it was not Christmastide, but Eastertide. And I was glad not to be alone. It was so warm that I was paddling, hand in hand, with my husband. It was our twelfth wedding anniversary. Another lone walker had met us that day too at the edge of the sands, and his greeting was, "Congratulations. Your honeymoon, I imagine."

I remember the delighted smiles with which we received that remark. So the first fine careless rapture of our love for each other had not been lost to us— or indeed on others.

As I thought about that April day nearly twenty five years ago, I was glad that in more ways than one it had been clear and unclouded. We had no notion of the trials and tragedies ahead. The thought of it helped me on this last Christmas Eve of the seventies to be able to get things in perspective.

I went on to think then of past Christmases. There was my very first in Scotland as a young bride. I was astonished, and indeed somewhat dismayed, to find that at that time Christmas day in Scotland was celebrated almost not at all. It was an ordinary working day. Tradespeople called, transport ran as usual, people went about their everyday business. It seemed that we were the sole household in the area celebrating in the traditional way. Everyone else was saving energy for the pagan festival of Hogmanay and New Year.

Some years later, when we had three children, things had not altered a lot. Big changes were to be made to our old-fashioned Manse, and part of the modernising was in the kitchen. To be away from the noise of the plumbers doing a normal day's work on Christmas day I had set our Christmas lunch upstairs in our large study. When I went downstairs to fetch the mince pies from the oven, I found cooker, pies—the lot—had departed. The plumbers had disconnected everything in the kitchen and I found the cooker with its festive fare residing unceremoniously in the backyard.

That was a joyous Christmas with fun and laughter, but those which followed were heavy with anxiety and grief. Our circle was incomplete the next year as Mike was in hospital and very ill. The following one was even sadder as my father died during Christmas night. The next was a bittersweet one which held unexpected joys (as related in "Be Still My Soul") but it was the last we should spend as a complete family, for my husband died soon after.

So it was that in a few short minutes on St. Andrews beach on the last Christmas Eve of the seventies my mind traversed many years. Time is a strange thing. When nothing special is happening, it seems to drag on endlessly and we say "That seemed like an eternity." When it is crevassed with sorrow or draped with joy we are inclined to say, "Time stood still." In fact, it is the other way about, is it not? That is when time takes on a new aspect and becomes part of eternity.

There on that sunlit beach with the waves sparkling and the sea birds calling, God was just a thought away.

Often at moments like that my particular ladder to Heaven is a beautiful poem or excerpt of prose which springs readily to mind. It has always been so since in my elementary school in Co. Antrim I was first aware of the emotions that beautiful words could arouse in me. Long before I understood the meaning, I was held spellbound by the words "multitudinous seas" and "in faery lands forlorn." My ladder to heaven this Christmas Eve as I looked towards the old, grey city of St. Andrews, was a poem about a different grey city.

A late lark twitters from the quiet skies;
And from the west,
Where the sun, his day's work ended,
Lingers as in content.
There falls on the old, gray city
An influence luminous and serene,
A shining peace.

The smoke ascends
In a rosy-and-golden haze. The spires
Shine, and are changed. In the valley

Shadows rise. The lark sings on. The sun,
Closing his benediction,
Sinks, and the darkening air
Thrills with a sense of the triumphing night—
Night with her train of stars
And her great gift of sleep.

So be my passing!
My task accomplished and the long day done,
My wages taken, and in my heart
Some late lark singing,
Let me be gathered to the quiet west,
The sundown splendid and serene,
Death.

W. E. Henley

This last Christmas Eve of the seventies was a very special one for us all. In our family gathering for the first time was Emma, a little eighteen months old girl of mixed race who a few months previously had been adopted by my daughter Rosalind and her husband Steve. During the early evening, after the setting of the sun, we walked with her and the rest of the family to the little old St. Leonard's Chapel in St. Andrews, the second of the two churches associated with the University. For the past six Christmas Eves we had gone there to take part in the family service conducted by Michael, my son, for the University families who were still around during the vacation. The small, building was always filled to overflowing and a large number of the congregation were children. The informal tone of the service was set in the first few minutes. Mike had just said that he hoped all the children were shortly going to help us with the carols, when a little five-year-old in front of me said to him, "But I only know Jingle Bells."

That Christmas Eve service was of special significance to us, as here in the same chapel where Rosalind and Steve had been married some four and a half years previously they were going to take their vows to bring up Emma in the Christian faith. Michael gave them a large Christmas candle afterwards to light for Emma every Christmas to remind her of the vows they had taken on her behalf.

So once again the season of goodwill and peace had its own personal meaning for me. That is why the first words of my anthology must be Christmas ones.

I think of the first Christmas I spent in Northern Ireland after the death of my husband. Our association with children can often enable us to feel the nearness and beauty of heavenly things. I was longing for this first Christmas of our bereavement to be over, for I guessed there would be many wistful longings and many heartaches as we looked at the vacant chair.

As Christmas drew near that year, I had gathered my class of eight-year-olds around me to tell them the story of the shepherds on the hills around Bethlehem. I had not at that time visited the shepherds' fields in the Holy Land. I went there a few years ago—to find that these open-air sites in Israel spoke to me more forcibly than the many shrines built around the holy places. With my eight-year-olds that first Christmas of our loss I had reached the part where the angel of the Lord had appeared to the shepherds and I had just said the words, "And then the angel said, . . ." when quite spontaneously the class recited in unison the words, "Fear not, for behold I bring you good tidings of great joy, which shall be to all people. For unto you is born this day in the city of David, a Saviour which is Christ the Lord." It is still difficult for me to put into words what that small incident meant to me. I seemed more aware than ever before of the heavenly radiance of that first Christmas in the fields beyond Bethlehem. Perhaps that is why many years later the shepherds' fields spoke so forcibly to me when I saw them.

Once I leave teaching I imagine that Christmas memories will often centre round the children in schools for whom I have compiled every year a Christmas anthology of word and song to be performed before their parents. Just because Christmas is such a social occasion we are in danger of losing much of its true meaning. Not so much, I think, because of all the myths and legends which have grown up around the Nativity. Not even in all the ruthless commercialising which seems to increase year after year about this time. The real danger is in reducing the whole thing to just a cosy little happening which took place nearly 2000 years ago. The danger is in trivialising it all.

How far is it to Bethlehem?
Not very far.
Shall we find the stable room
Lit by a star?

If we touch His tiny hand
Will He awake?
Will He know we've come so far
Just for His sake?

Well, how far will we really have come? Maybe it's all a bit farther than we think, for the significance of Bethlehem can only be realised if we take the trouble to travel by Jerusalem and Calvary. We shall not really see the meaning of the child in the crib unless we spend some time pondering on what happened to him thirty years later. A little baby throws out his arms in the crib and in his outstretched arms we have a cameo of Calvary.

I expect Mary the mother often asked how far they had still to go. It was all of eighty rough miles from Nazareth to Bethlehem—but it was more, far more than that. It was a journey in humility and suffering as well as in adoration and joy. Even in the sublime statements in the Song of Mary which we call the Magnificat, there is the very stuff of revolution. He has filled those that are hungry. The rich he has sent empty away. He will cast down the mighty. He will exalt the humble. The blessedness which came to Mary was just the prelude to the sword which would pierce her heart thirty years later.

I expect those shepherds coming down off the night shift to look for the Infant King would also say, "How far must we go?" And when they reached the stable which was probably just a cave, before they could enter to see him they would have to stoop down. Bethlehem is as far as that kind of humility.

Every year we say again, "Well, I wonder what really happened that first Christmas?" If we take the exquisite story as it is told in Luke's Gospel, can we possibly separate the prophecy from the history and the history from the symbolism? They are so intermingled that it's just not possible to separate them. And perhaps we are not meant to. For every account, whether historical or not, is valuable in its own way. It can make some aspect of truth known. Indeed it will be the very essence of saving truth if it points us the way to Christ.

Some years ago in one of my broadcasts I told a true story of a little girl, Ruth, who was being left in the care of a baby-sitter, much to her consternation. She was protesting very loudly and her mother was becoming more and more exasperated. Finally she said, "Ruth, I don't really know what you're making all the fuss about. You know that I've always told you that even when I'm not here, God is always with you."

That really put the tin lid on it. The child screamed in fury. "I don't want God. I want somebody with skin on."

It is I think not irreverent to say that that gives us something of a clue as to what happened that first Christmas. We sing in our carols

> Veiled in flesh the Godhead see,
> Hail the Incarnate Deity.

The old hymn books had it as *wrapped* in flesh the Godhead see. That is what happened that first Christmas. We are allowed to find our God there—with skin on.

We can sieve through all the historical facts; collect all the information of time, place and date; we can discard all the legendary details here and there; and at the end of it all we may well have a useful bit of argumentation and documentation. But it could all be colourless and arid if we have missed the central truth of Christmas. Our human spirits cry out to know something more than just an historical figure, or just an eternal idea or an abstract Creator. We want to find God and to know what He is like.

The loveliest name given to Jesus is I think Emmanuel—*God with us*. Something which was not available to us before that first Christmas became available. The distant God came near. The simple narrative of Bethlehem is not related just to give us roughly the information of what happened historically. It is to lay bare for us the reality of God. In Jesus we see, as nowhere else, the love, compassion and mercy and purity of God. The redemption of the world is wrapped in swaddling clothes.

Little man and God indeed,
Little and poor Thou art all we need.
We will follow where Thou dost lead
And we will heed
Our brother Son of Mary.

Christmas Carol

Come, worship the King
That little white thing
Asleep on His mother's soft breast
Ye bright stars bow down
Weave for him a crown
Christ Jesus by angels confessed.

Come, children and peep
But hush ye, and creep
On tiptoe to where the Babe lies;
Then whisper His name
And lo! like a flame
The glory light shines in His eyes.

Come, strong men and see
This high mystery
Tread firm where the shepherds have trod,
And watch, 'mid the hair
Of the maiden so fair
The five little fingers of God.

Come, old men and grey
The star leads the way
It halts and your wanderings cease;
Look down on His face
Then filled with His grace
Depart ye, God's servants, in peace.

Studdert Kennedy

Christmas

All Paradise
Collected in one bud
Doth sweetly rise
From its fair virgin bed
Omnipotence an infant's shape puts on
Immensity becomes a little one.

Joseph Beaumont

A Christmas Verse

He had no royal palace—
Only a stable bare.

He had no watchful servants—
An ox and ass stood there.

But light shone forth from where He lay
The King of Love upon the hay.

A Christmas Wish

To every hearth a little fire
To every board a little feast,
To every heart a joy,
To every child a toy,
Shelter for bird and beast.

Rose Fyleman

Christmas Eve

On Christmas Eve my mother read
The story once again
Of how the little Child was born
And of the three Wise men.

And how by following the Star
They found Him where He lay
And brought Him gifts; and that is why
We keep our Christmas day.

And when she read it all, I went
And looked across the snow
And thought of Jesus coming
As He did so long ago.

I looked into the East and saw
A great star blazing bright;
There were three men upon the road
All black against the light.

I thought I heard the angels sing
Away upon the hill. . . .
I held my breath . . . it seemed as if
The whole great world were still.

It seemed to me the little Child
Was being born again. . . .
And very near . . . and THEN somehow
Was NOW . . . or NOW was THEN!

Edna Kingsley Wallace

Christmas is a time for dreaming. We all give way to the child
in us and do a bit of guessing as to what might be in that package
hung on the Christmas tree and labelled with our name. Those
who don't dream much at other times indulge their fancy when
they wonder what Christmas morn will bring, even though
growing up means realising that to avoid over-expectation is the
beginning of wisdom. Yet I believe we should dream. C. S. Lewis
once said that because a child dreams of enchanted woods and
trees, that does not make him despise real woods. The real
woods when he returned to them would be a little bit enchanted
just because he had dreamt of fairy woods.

The months before that first Christmas were times of dreaming
too. Mary and Joseph had their visions; and great truths were
revealed to them about a coming Saviour. Those were wonderful
dreams, enchanted dreams, but the one which came to Joseph
after the birth had less enchantment. It told them to prepare for a
flight into Egypt as death was already threatening.

A lovely story was written by a Northern Irish Presbyterian minister for broadcasting some years ago about three trees which dreamed and talked to each other as they grew together on a hillside. The first tree wished to be cut down and made into a baby's cradle. The second wished to be made into a wonderful ship carrying rich goods and precious jewels. The third didn't particularly wish to be cut down but just wanted to go on growing on the hillside, pointing its branches up to heaven.

As the time passed the woodcutters came along, and the tree which had wished so much to be a baby's cradle was made into a cattle stall. And it was there that Jesus was born. The second tree which had wished so much to be a splendid ship was cut down and made into a small fishing boat which was eventually bought by Simon Peter and later lent to Jesus so that He could speak to the people on the shores of Galilee. And the third tree, which had just wanted to go on growing had to be cut down, because it was needed as a cross of shame. But it was the cross on which Christ the Saviour of the world died—the same Christ who was the babe in the cattle stall; the same Christ who taught from Simon Peter's boat.

Our dreams are never better for us than what God wills for us. If they don't come true then what in the end happens may be far, far better than ever we dreamed.

The Oxen

Christmas Eve and twelve of the clock.
"Now they are all on their knees,"
An elder said as we sat in a flock
By the embers in hearthside ease.

We pictured the meek, mild creatures where
They dwelt in their strawy pen,
Nor did it occur to one of us there
To doubt they were kneeling then.

So fair a fancy few would weave
In these years! Yet I feel,
If someone said on Christmas Eve,
"Come; see the oxen kneel

"In the lonely barton by yonder coomb
Our childhood used to know,"
I should go with him in the gloom
Hoping it might be so.

                                        Thomas Hardy

A Christmas Carol

The holly wreath that now
Our house adorns
Will wither soon and be
A jagged crown of thorns;

Nor when fir needles fall
Can tinsel hide
The grey and naked limbs
Of the tree crucified;

The fair feast of Christmas
Our flesh enthrones
Even as we gaze piles up
A hollow heap of bones;

By which I know a sad
And doleful thing
That though we eat and drink
And gladsome carols sing

The ancient curse still blights
The human tree
And things men touch become
Shadows of Calvary.

                                        Fred Cogswell

Christ Child

Warm as a little mouse he lay,
Hay kept him from the winter's harm
Bleating of puzzled lamb he heard,
And voices from the nearby farm.

His mother's eyes were bent on him
As to her frozen breast he clung;
His father stopped the draughty cracks
And sang a merry herding song.

Who would have thought upon that hour
Those little hands might stay a plague,
Those eyes would quell a multitude,
That voice would still a rising wave?

Only the omens of the night,
The lowing ox, the moaning tree,
Hinted the cruelty to come;
A raven croaked, "Gethsemane."

Henry Treece

Christmas

An azure sky
All star-bestrewn.
A lowly crib,
A hushèd room.
An open door,
A hill afar,
Where little lambs
And shepherds are.

To such a world
On such a night,
Came Jesus—
Little Lord of Light.

Source unknown

The Present Tense
Your holy hearsay is not evidence
Give me the good news in the present tense.

What happened nineteen hundred years ago
May not have happened; how am I to know?

The living truth is what I long to see,
I cannot lean upon what used to be.

So shut the Bible up and show me how
The Christ you talk about is living now.

                                   Sydney Carter

The wise men ask
"What language did Christ speak?"
They cavil, argue, search and little prove.
O sages, leave your Syriac and your Greek!
Each heart contains the knowledge that you seek;
Christ spoke the universal language—LOVE!

> Love ever lives
> Forgives
> Outlives,
> Ever stands
> With open hands,
> And while it lives
> It gives
> For this is Love's prerogative
> To give
> And give
> And give.

Christmas

The bells of waiting Advent ring,
The Tortoise stove is lit again
And lamp-oil light across the night
Has caught the streaks of winter rain
In many a stained-glass window sheen
From Crimson Lake to Hooker's Green.

The holly in the windy hedge
And round the Manor House the yew
Will soon be stripped to deck the ledge,
The altar, font and arch and pew,
So that the villagers can say
"The church looks nice" on Christmas Day.

Provincial public houses blaze
And Corporation tramcars clang,
On lighted tenements I gaze
Where paper decorations hang,
And bunting in the red Town Hall
Says "Merry Christmas to you all."

And London shops on Christmas Eve
Are strung with silver bells and flowers
As hurrying clerks the City leave
To pigeon-haunted classic towers,
And marbled clouds go scudding by
The many-steepled London sky.

And girls in slacks remember Dad,
And oafish louts remember Mum,
And sleepless children's hearts are glad
And Christmas morning bells say, "Come!"
Even to shining ones who dwell
Safe in the Dorchester Hotel.

And is it true? And is it true?
This most tremendous tale of all,
Seen in a stained-glass window's hue,
A Baby in an ox's stall?
The Maker of the stars and sea
Became a Child on earth for me?

And is it true? For if it is
No loving fingers tying strings
Around those tissued fripperies,
The sweet and silly Christmas things,
Bath salts and inexpensive scent
And hideous tie so kindly meant,

No love that in a family dwells
No carolling in frosty air,
Nor all the steeple-shaking bells
Can with this single Truth compare—
That God was Man in Palestine
And lives today in Bread and Wine.

John Betjeman

Some searching words were written by Ogden Nash in 1938 when war was on the horizon.

"Merry Christmas! NEARLY everybody!" From "I'm a Stranger Here Myself"

> People can't concentrate properly
> On blowing other people to pieces properly
> If their minds are poisoned
> By thoughts suitable to the 25th of December.

One Solitary Life
A quotation from a Hamilton, Ontario newspaper.

Here is a man who was born of Jewish parents in an obscure village, the child of a peasant woman. He grew up in another obscure village. He worked in a carpenter's shop until he was thirty, and then for three years he was an itinerant preacher.

He never wrote a book, he never held an office, he never owned a home. He never had a family. He never went to college. He never put his foot inside a big city. He never travelled two hundred miles from the place where he was born. He never did one of these things that usually accompany greatness. He had no credentials but himself.

He had nothing to do with this world except the naked power of his manhood. While still a young man, the tide of popular opinion turned against Him. His friends ran away. One of them denied Him. He was turned over to His enemies. He went through the mockery of a trial.

He was nailed to a cross between two thieves. His executioners gambled for the only piece of property he had on earth, while he was dying—and that was his coat. When he was dead he was taken down and laid in a borrowed grave, through the pity of a friend.

Nineteen wide centuries have come and gone, and today He is the centrepiece of the human race, and the leader of the column of progress. I am far within the mark when I say that all the armies that ever marched, and all the navies that were ever built, and all the parliaments that ever sat, and all the kings that ever reigned, put together, have not affected the life of man upon earth as powerfully as has that solitary life.

Jimmy Reid: "If there is a God, I hope that it will be Jesus."

Ex Ore Infantium

Little Jesus, wast Thou shy
Once, and just so small as I?
And what did it feel like to be
Out of Heaven and just like me?
Didst Thou sometimes think of *there*,
And ask where all the angels were?
I should think that I would cry
For my house all made of sky;
I would look about the air,
And wonder where my angels were;
And at waking 'twould distress me—
Not an angel there to dress me.

Hadst Thou ever any toys,
Like us little girls and boys?
And didst Thou play in Heaven with all
The angels, that were not too tall,
With stars for marbles? Did the things
Play, 'Can you see me?' through their wings?

Didst Thou kneel at night to pray,
And didst Thou join Thy hands, this way?
And did they tire sometimes, being young,
And make the prayer seem very long?
And dost Thou like it best that we
Should join our hands to pray to Thee?
I used to think before I knew,
The prayer not said unless we do.
And did Thy Mother at the night
Kiss Thee, and fold the clothes in right?
And didst Thou feel quite good in bed,
Kissed, and sweet, and Thy prayers said?

Thou canst not have forgotten all
That it feels like to be small:

And Thou know'st I cannot pray
To Thee in my father's way—
When Thou wast so little, say,
Couldst Thou talk Thy Father's way?

So, a little Child, come down
And hear a child's tongue like Thy own;
Take me by the hand and walk,
And listen to my baby-talk.
To Thy Father show my prayer
(He will look, Thou art so fair)
And say, 'O Father, I, Thy Son,
Bring the prayer of a little one.'

And He will smile, that children's tongue
Has not changed since Thou wast young!

Francis Thompson

The Lamb

Little lamb, who made thee?
Dost thou know who made thee?
Gave thee life and bade thee feed
By the stream and o'er the mead;
Gave thee clothing of delight,
Softest clothing, woolly, bright;
Gave thee such a tender voice,
Making all the vales rejoice?
Little lamb, who made thee?
Dost thou know who made thee?

Little lamb, I'll tell thee,
Little lamb, I'll tell thee:
He is callèd by thy name,
For He calls Himself a lamb.
He is meek and He is mild;
He became a little child.
I a child, and thou a lamb,
We are all callèd by His name.
Little lamb, God bless thee!
Little lamb, God bless thee!

William Blake

Joseph

Who has not carolled Mary
And who her praise would dim?
But what of humble Joseph
Is there no song for him?

If Joseph had not driven
Straight nails through honest wood;
If Joseph had not cherished
His Mary as he should;

If Joseph had not proved him
A sire both kind and wise
Would he have drawn with favour
The Child's all-probing eyes?

Would Christ have prayed "Our Father"
Or cried that name on death,
Unless He first had honoured
Joseph of Nazareth?

Gilbert Thomas

Bethlehem

When the herd were watching
In the midnight chill
Came a spotless lambkin
From the Heavenly hill.

Snow was on the mountain
And the wind was cold
When from God's own garden
Dropped a rose of gold.

When 'twas bitter winter
Houseless and forlorn
In a star-lit stable
Christ the Babe was born

Welcome, heavenly lambkin;
Welcome, golden rose;
Alleluia, Baby,
In the swaddling clothes.

William Canton

Moonless darkness stands between,
Past, O past, no more be seen!
But the Bethlehem star may lead me
To the sight of Him who freed me
From the self that I have been.
Make me pure, Lord; Thou art holy;
Make me meek, Lord; Thou wert lowly;
Now beginning and alway;
Now begin, on Christmas day.

Gerard Manley Hopkins

I was very young—still at primary school—when for some reason or other my attention was drawn to the next poem, which is not really a familiar Christmas poem for a young child to learn. I remember, however, committing it to heart and reciting it to another of my young friends when she came round to play at "houses" with our dolls in the first very humble home I ever lived in. I can still see the kitchen with its plain furniture, the fire in the old-fashioned hearth, and her rather bewildered face as I said this rather adult poem to her. She must have thought I was intolerably priggish. Yet I still love the poem.

Preparations

Yet if His Majesty, our Sovereign Lord,
Should of his own accord
Friendly himself invite,
And say, "I'll be your guest tomorrow night,"
How should we stir ourselves, call and command
All hands to work! "Let no man idle stand!

"Set me fine Spanish tables in the hall;
See they be fitted all;
Let there be room to eat

And order taken that there want no meat.
See every sconce and candlestick made bright,
That without tapers they may give a light.

curtains "Look to the presence; are the carpets spread,
The dazie o'er the head,
The cushions in the chairs,
And all the candles lighted on the stairs?
Perfume the chambers, and in any case
Let each man give attendance in his place!"

Thus if the king were coming would we do;
And 'twere good reason too;
For 'tis a duteous thing
To show all honour to an earthly king,
And after all our travail and our cost,
So he be pleased, to think no labour lost.

But at the coming of the King of Heaven
All's set at six and seven;
We wallow in our sin,
Christ can not find a chamber in the inn.
We entertain Him always like a stranger,
And as at first, still lodge Him in the manger.

Journey of the Magi

"A cold coming we had of it,
Just the worst time of the year
For a journey, and such a long journey:
The ways deep and the weather sharp,
The very dead of winter."
And the camels galled, sore-footed, refractory,
Lying down in the melting snow.
There were times we regretted
The summer palaces on slopes, the terraces,
And the silken girls bringing sherbet.
Then the camel men cursing and grumbling
And running away, and wanting their liquor and women.
And the night fires going out, and the lack of shelters,
And the cities hostile, and the towns unfriendly

And the villages dirty and charging high prices:
A hard time we had of it.
At the end we preferred to travel all night,
Sleeping in snatches,
With the voices singing in our ears, saying
That this was all folly.

Then at dawn we came down to a temperate valley,
Wet, below the snow-line, smelling of vegetation,
With a running stream and a water-mill beating the darkness,
And three trees on the low sky.
And an old white horse galloped away in the meadow.
Then we came to a tavern with vine leaves over the lintel,
Six hands at an open door dicing for pieces of silver,
And feet kicking the empty wine-skins.
But there was no information, so we continued
And arrived at evening, not a moment too soon
Finding the place; it was (you may say) satisfactory.

All this was a long time ago, I remember,
And I would do it again, but set down
This set down
This; were we led all that way for
Birth or Death? There was a Birth, certainly,
We had evidence and no doubt. I had seen birth and death
But had thought they were different; this Birth was
Hard and bitter agony for us, like Death, our death.
We returned to our places, these Kingdoms,
But no longer at ease here, in the old dispensation,
With an alien people clutching their gods.
I should be glad of another death.

                                                    T. S. Eliot

The Journey of the Magi

THIS IS THE STORY unearthed by Marco Polo in the late 13th
century. During his travels throughout the world he searched for
much obscure information, and part of his search was for the lost

chronicles of the astrologer Sufi Abbas. After he had found the faded and tattered rolls of parchment for which he had been searching, he used to relate the story to his three daughters, and little by little the following myth took shape.

Gaspar, King of Tarshish was black as ebony, young, tall and handsome.

Balthazar, King of Ancient Chaldea, was middle-aged and of medium height and olive complexion.

Melchior, King of Nubia, was into old age, infirm and withered and shrunken in stature, pale as death.

They set out to follow the Star, to find this new King who had been foretold. On one point only were they agreed—they were looking for someone noble, regal and wise. But each was expecting a King with the same colour of skin as his own. At first they reasoned quietly about it, but as the journey progressed they became angry and contentious. The glory of the light of the Star they were following dimmed as they wrangled and disputed. Only when they became secretly ashamed of their warfare of words and sought again the early companionship they had enjoyed, did the star shine brightly again.

Then they talked of what their secret aspirations were regarding their quest and where it would lead them. Gaspar the young and energetic monarch felt that above all, the world needed a sovereign lord. He showed the royal gift he had brought—the gift of gold for a truly royal personage.

Balthazar the middle-aged monarch felt that no earthly sovereign lord was sufficient. He longed for a revelation of God Himself and so he had brought a gift of frankincense signifying worship.

Melchior the old man, nearing as he knew the end of his life, dwelt on years past, with things left undone that he wished he had done, and things done that he wished could be erased. What he was searching for was a Saviour. He instinctively knew that such a Saviour would also be a sufferer. So he took with him his gift of myrhh.

Eventually they arrived at Bethlehem only to be overcome with chagrin and dismay, for the Star had led them to a baby cradled in a mother's arms as she sang. They all three listened.

"My soul doth magnify the Lord!" she sang.

"The LORD!" exclaimed Gaspar. "Then I have found my Sovereign Lord." And he offered his gift of gold.

Mary sang on. "And my spirit hath rejoiced in God. . . ."

"In GOD!" called out Balthazar. "My search is ended." And he gave his gift of incense to the Babe.

Mary's song continued. "My soul doth magnify the Lord and my spirit hath rejoiced in God my Saviour."

"My SAVIOUR" echoed Melchior. And he presented his gift of myrrh.

So Gaspar found the Sovereign Lord for whom he had been searching. Balthazar recognised in Jesus the God for whom he had been seeking, and Melchior the Saviour who he realised, was his greatest need.

> In The Bleak Mid-Winter
> What can I give Him,
> Poor as I am?
> If I were a shepherd
> I would give a lamb;
> If I were a wise man,
> I would do my part,
> Yet what I can I give Him,
> Give my heart.

Christina Rossetti

> The Family Sitting
>
> In the days of Caesar Augustus
> There went forth this decree:
> Si quis rectus et justus
> Liveth in Galilee
> Let him go up to Jerusalem
> And pay his scot to me.
>
> There are passed one after the other
> Christmases fifty-three,
> Since I sat here with my mother
> And heard the great decree:
> How they went up to Jerusalem
> Out of Galilee,

They have passed one after the other,
Father and mother died,
Brother and sister and brother
Taken and sanctified.
I am left alone in the sitting,
With none to sit beside.

On the fly-leaves of these old prayer-books
The childish writings fade,
Which show that once they were their books
In the days when prayer was made
For other kings and princesses
William and Adelaide.

The pillars are twisted with holly,
And the font is wreathed with yew.
Christ forgive me for folly,
Youth's lapses—not a few,
For the hardness of my middle life,
For age's fretful view.

Cotton-wool letters on scarlet,
All the ancient lore,
Tell how the chieftains starlit
To Bethlehem came to adore;
To hail Him King in the manger,
Wonderful, Counsellor.

The bells ring out in the steeple
The gladness of erstwhile,
And the children of other people
Are walking up the aisle;
They brush my elbow in passing,
Some turn to give me a smile.

Is the almond-blossom bitter?
Is the grasshopper heavy to bear?
Christ, make me happier, fitter
To go to my own over there:

Jerusalem the Golden,
What bliss beyond compare!

My Lord, where I have offended
Do Thou forgive it me.
That so, when all being ended,
I hear Thy last decree,
I may go up to Jerusalem
Out of Galilee.

John Meade Falkner

The next three items in my Christmas anthology are really
Christmas hymns. The third is universally known and loved. It
was written by Cecil Frances Alexander in the city of
Londonderry not too far away from the county of Antrim where I
was born and lived the early years of my life. Worldwide this
carol is associated with the processional, leading up to the service
of Nine Lessons and Carols. I shall always think of it as the
moving beginning to the Carol event in my own little rural
school. Some seventy very young children walked in to their
seats year by year singing as they walked, "Once in Royal
David's City." By the time they had reached the last verse "And
our eyes at last shall see Him" they were standing, faces shining
and earnest, looking towards their parents and friends. I have
heard very many moving carols in my time, but none has ever
moved me so much as the uninhibited sweet and natural singing
of my pupils in this lovely hymn.

The two songs which precede it I found to my great delight a
few Christmases ago. I had a very rumbustious class, nearly all
boys, who definitely were not much good at singing soft lullabies.
But they did enjoy singing gleefully the first song to "Weel may
the keel row" and the second to "John Brown's Body."

When God Almighty came to be one of us,
Masking the glory of His golden train,
Dozens of plain things kindled by accident,
And they will never be the same again.
Sing all you midwives, dance all you carpenters,
Sing all the publicans and shepherds too,

God in His mercy uses the commonplace,
God on His birthday had a need of you.

Splendour of Rome and Local Authority,
Working on policy with furrowed head,
Joined to locate Messiah's Nativity,
Just where the prophets had already said.
Sing all you taxmen, dance the Commissioners,
Sing civil servants and policemen too,
God in His purpose, uses the governments,
God on His birthday had a need of you.

Wise men they called them, earnest astrologers,
Watching for meaning in the moving stars.
Science or fancy, learnèd or laughable,
Theirs was a vision that was brought to pass.
Sing all you wise men, dance all the scientists,
Whether your theories are false or true,
God uses knowledge, God uses ignorance,
God on His birthday had a need of you.

Sing, all creation, made for his purposes,
Called by His providence to live and move:
None is unwanted, none insignificant,
Love needs a universe of folk to love.
Old men and maidens, young men and children,
Black ones and coloured ones and white ones too.
God on His birthday, and to eternity,
God took upon Himself the need of you.

Michael Hewlett

Come sing the praise of Jesus, sing His love with hearts aflame,
Sing His wondrous birth of Mary when to save the world He
came.
Tell the life He lived for others and His mighty deeds proclaim,
For Jesus Christ is King.
　Praise and glory be to Jesus
　For Jesus Christ is King.

When His foes arose and slew Him, He was victor in the fight,
Over death and Hell He triumphed in His Resurrection might,

He has raised our fallen manhood and enthroned it in the height,
For Jesus Christ is King.

There's a joy for all who serve Him more than human tongue can
say,
There is pardon for the sinner and the night is turned to day,
There is healing for our sorrows, there is music all the way,
For Jesus Christ is King.

We will witness to His glory and will spread His love abroad,
We will cleave the hosts of darkness with the Spirit's piercing
sword,
We will lead the souls in prison to the freedom of the Lord,
For Jesus Christ is King.

David's City

Once in royal David's city
Stood a lowly cattle shed,
Where a mother laid her baby
In a manger for His bed;
Mary was that mother mild,
Jesus Christ her little child.

He came down to earth from heaven
Who is God and Lord of all,
And His shelter was a stable
And His cradle was a stall;
With the poor and mean and lowly
Lived on earth our Saviour holy.

And through all His wondrous childhood
He would honour and obey,
Love, and watch the lowly maiden
In whose gentle arms He lay:
Christian children all must be
Mild, obedient, good as He.

For He is our childhood's pattern:
Day by day like us He grew;
He was little, weak and helpless
Tears and smiles like us He knew,
And He feeleth for our sadness
And He shareth in our gladness.

And our eyes at last shall see Him,
Through His own redeeming love;
For that child so dear and gentle
Is our Lord in heaven above;
And He leads His children on
To the place where He has gone.

Not in that poor lowly stable,
With the oxen standing by,
We shall see Him, but in heaven,
Set at God's right hand on high;
When like stars, His children crowned,
All in white shall wait around.

Cecil F. Alexander

There are two unusual little carols which we have enjoyed singing at our carol events. The younger pupils loved the charm and simplicity of *The Cat and Mouse Carol*, words and music by Ted Hutchinson.

Said the cat to the mouse, in their dark little house,
In that stable so long ago,
"I am wondering why that bright star in the sky
Is shining upon us down below."

And the night skies rang as the angels sang,
When Love came down to earth
And the night skies rang as the angels sang,
When the Baby King had His Birth.

Said the mouse to the cat as in wonder they sat,
And they saw Mary's face filled with joy,
"Perhaps that star we can see is to tell you and me,
Of the coming of this precious little boy."
And the night skies . . . .

Sleepy shepherds they saw as they crept through the door
And they brought little gifts to the Child.
As they gazed with love on the child from above
Mary turned to the shepherds and smiled.
And the night skies . . . .

So they happily sat, little mouse, little cat,
As they heard Mary singing to her son,
As she cradles with care, little Jesus so fair,
This baby, the Lord's chosen one.
And the night skies . . . .

My rumbustious boys helped make up the words to a wagoner's song tune, and they did enjoy placing their recorders, whistling and singing for Jesus.

> I drive my little donkey
> Across the country wide
> It pulls my little wagon
> With gifts for Christ inside.
> For Bethlehem I'm steering
> To see the new-born King
> I'll play my pipe for Jesus
> I'll whistle and I'll sing.
>
> I've travelled far to see Him
> On this my Lord's birthday,
> My humble gifts I've offered
> And now I'm on my way.
> From Bethlehem I'm leaving
> I've seen the new-born King
> I'll play my pipe for Jesus
> I'll whistle and I'll sing.

WAGONER'S SONG

I   drive my little   donkey A-   cross the country

wide It   pulls my little   wagon with   gifts for Christ in

side For   Bethlehem I'm steering to see the new-born King I'll

whistle

play my pipe for   Jesus I'll   whistle and I'll   sing

and play recorders here

The following little carol I made up and sang to my own children when they were very small. I do not suppose they remember it and it has not seen the light of day since they were tiny.

Mary's Song For The Baby Jesus
Words and Music by Elizabeth Urch.

Sleep my baby, gently sleep
While the shepherds keep their sheep.
Overhead the stars are bright
Shedding o'er the earth their light.
In a manger now you lie
Sent to me from God on high,
Sent to me from God on high.

Sleep my baby, gently sleep
While the shepherds keep their sheep.
Baby Jesus, Holy One,
Thou art God's beloved Son.
Yet a manger is your bed
And no pillow for your head,
And no pillow for your head.

Sleep my baby, gently sleep
While the shepherds keep their sheep.
I will watch o'er Thee this night
Watch o'er Thee, my Life, my Light,
Saviour Jesus, King Thou art,
Yet my Babe, close to my heart,
Yet my Babe close to my heart.

MARY'S SONG FOR THE BABY JESUS

Sleep my ba-by gent-ly slee-p While the shep-herds keep their

sheep: Ov-er –head the stars are bright Shed-ding o'er the earth their

light In a man-ger now you lie Sent to me   from God on

high Sent to me from God on   high.

My soul doth magnify the Lord,
And my Spirit hath rejoiced in God my Saviour.
For He hath regarded the low estate of His handmaiden;
For, behold, from henceforth all generations shall call me blessed.
For he that is mighty hath done to me great things;
And holy is his name.
And his mercy is on them that fear him
From generation to generation.
He hath shewed strength with his arm; He hath scattered the proud in the imagination of their hearts.
He hath put down the mighty from their seats, and exalted them of low degree.
He hath filled the hungry with good things; and the rich he hath sent empty away.
He hath holpen his servant Israel, in remembrance of his mercy;
As he spake to our fathers, to Abraham and to his seed for ever.

Luke 1:46-55

FOR UNTO US A CHILD IS BORN, UNTO US A SON IS GIVEN:
AND THE GOVERNMENT SHALL BE UPON HIS SHOULDER:
AND HIS NAME SHALL BE CALLED
WONDERFUL
  COUNSELLOR
    THE MIGHTY GOD
      THE EVERLASTING FATHER,
        THE PRINCE OF PEACE.

—Isaiah 9: 6

I gratefully acknowledge permission to reproduce copyright poems in this book.

Sir John Betjeman and his publishers John Murray Ltd. for *Christmas*.

Sydney Carter and Stainer and Bell Ltd. for *The Present Tense* from Greenprint for Song. Galaxy Music Corporation, New York for U.S.A. rights.

Thomas Stearns Eliot's executors and Faber and Faber Ltd. for *Journey Of the Magi* from Collected Poems (1909—1962) by T. S. Eliot.
Also copyright 1936 by Harcourt, Brace, Jouancuitch Inc. (c) 1963, 1964 by T. S. Eliot. Reprinted by permission of Harcourt, Brace, Jouanovitch Inc., U.S.A.

Rose Fyleman's executors and The Society of Authors for *A Christmas Wish* originally published by Methuen.

Michael Hewlett and Stainer and Bell Ltd. for *When God Almighty Came To Be One Of Us* taken from Faith, Folk and Festivity. Galaxy Music Corporation, New York for U.S.A. rights.

Ted Hutchinson and Chappell International Music Publishers Ltd. for words and music of *The Cat and The Mouse* Carol (c) 1974, E.F.D.S. Publications Ltd. Assigned 1978 to Chappell International Music Publishers Ltd. Reproduced by kind permission of Chappell Music Ltd.

Ogden Nash's executors and A. P. Watt Ltd. for *Merry Christmas, Nearly Everybody*.

Gilbert Thomas's Executors and David and Charles Ltd. for *Joseph* from Gilbert Thomas Collected Poems, David and Charles.

Henry Treece and Faber and Faber Ltd. for *Christ Child* from The Black Seasons by Henry Treece.

Edna Kingsley Wallace's executors and Elsevier-Dutton Publishing Co. Inc. for *Christmas Eve* from Feelings and Things by Edna Kingsley Wallace. Copyright 1916 by E. P. Dutton and Co. Inc. Renewal copyright 1944, by Edna Kingsley Wallace.

Whilst every effort has been made to secure permissions, in a few cases it has proved impossible to trace the author or his executor. I apologise for any omission and shall redress this if brought to my notice.

E. U.

CHRISTMAS

Titles and First Lines. Titles in Capitals.

Page

"A cold coming we had of it 27
A late lark twitters 9
All Paradise collected in one bud 15
An azure sky all star-bestrewn 19

BETHLEHEM 25

Christmas Eve and twelve of the clock 17
Come sing the praise of Jesus 33
Come, worship the King 14
CAT AND MOUSE CAROL, THE 36
CHRIST CHILD 18
CHRISTMAS (Beaumont) 15
CHRISTMAS (Betjeman) 20
CHRISTMAS (Source unknown) 19
CHRISTMAS CAROL (Kennedy) 14
CHRISTMAS CAROL, A (Cogswell) 18
CHRISTMAS EVE 15
CHRISTMAS VERSE, A 15
CHRISTMAS WISH, A 15

DAVID'S CITY 34
DONKEY CAROL 38

EX ORE INFANTIUM 23

FAMILY SITTING, THE 30
For unto us a Child is born 42

He had no royal palace 15
Here is a man who was born 22

I drive my little donkey 38
IN THE BLEAK MID-WINTER 30
In the days of Caesar Augustus 30

JOSEPH 25
JOURNEY OF THE MAGI (Eliot) 27
JOURNEY OF THE MAGI (Marco Polo) 28

LAMB, THE 24
Little Jesus, wast Thou shy 23
Little lamb, who made thee 24
Love ever lives 20

MAGNIFICAT 42
MARY'S SONG FOR THE BABY JESUS 40
Merry Christmas! NEARLY everybody! 22
Moonless darkness stands between 26
My soul doth magnify the Lord 42

Once in royal David's city 34
On Christmas Eve my mother read 15
ONE SOLITARY LIFE 22
OXEN, THE 17

PREPARATIONS 26
PRESENT TENSE, THE 19

Said the cat to the mouse 36
Sleep my baby, gently sleep 40

The bells of waiting Advent 20
The holly wreath that now 18
The wise men ask 20
To every hearth a little fire 15

WAGONER'S SONG .... 38 & 39
Warm as a little mouse he lay 18
What can I give Him 30
When God Almighty came to be one of us 32
When the herd were watching 25
Who has not carolled Mary 25

Yet if His Majesty, our sovereign Lord 26
Your holy hearsay is not evidence 19

LIST OF AUTHORS

Christmas

ALEXANDER, CECIL FRANCES...............................35

BEAUMONT, JOSEPH 15
BETJEMAN, SIR JOHN 21
BLAKE, WILLIAM 24

CANTON, WILLIAM 26
CARTER, SYDNEY 20
COGSWELL, FRED 18

ELIOT, THOMAS STEARNS 28

FALKNER, JOHN MEADE 32
FYLEMAN, ROSE AMY 15

HARDY, THOMAS 18
HENLEY, WILLIAM ERNEST 10
HEWLETT, MICHAEL 33
HOPKINS, GERARD MANLEY 26
HUTCHINSON, TED 36

KENNEDY, STUDDERT 14

NASH, OGDEN 22

ROSSETTI, CHRISTINA 30

THOMAS, GILBERT 25
THOMPSON, FRANCIS 24
TREECE, HENRY 19

URCH, ELIZABETH 40

WALLACE, EDNA KINGSLEY 16